A Child's Story of
Thanksgiving

By Laura J. Rader
Illustrated by Mary Ann Utt

ideals children's books™
Nashville, Tennessee

ISBN 0-8249-5327-4

Published by Ideals Children's Books
An imprint of Ideals Publications
A division of Guideposts
535 Metroplex Drive, Suite 250
Nashville, Tennessee 37211
www.idealspublications.com

The Library of Congress has already catalogued this book as follows:
Rader, Laura.
    A child's story of Thanksgiving / by Laura Rader ; illustrated by Mary Ann
Utt.—1st ed.
       p.   cm.
  Summary: Briefly chronicles Thanksgiving celebrations from fifteenth century Massachusetts to the present.
    1. Thanksgiving Day–Juvenile literature. [1. Thanksgiving Day.] I. Utt, Mary Ann.   II. Title.
GT4975.R33   1998
394.2649—dc21

                                                                                        98-16611

Printed and bound in Mexico by RR Donnelley & Sons.

To Mama, and in memory of Grandma, who taught me to love reading and books. —L.J.R.

To Mom and Dad. —M.A.U.

10 8 6 4 2 1 3 5 7 9

Everyone thinks of turkey, cranberry sauce, and pumpkin pie at Thanksgiving. These are important to our traditional Thanksgiving celebration. But Thanksgiving Day is about more than just eating a big meal.

A long time ago, King James I of England said that every English man and woman must join the same church or leave the country. A group of people called Puritans would not join this church. They wanted to worship God the way they wanted to.

Because of this, many Puritans were put into prison. Some were even hanged. Finally, a group of Puritans sneaked out of England and moved to Holland.

The Puritans were not happy living in Holland. They were farmers, and there was not enough land in Holland for farming. The Puritans wanted to make a life for themselves in a new land.

In 1620, a group of one hundred men, women, and children set sail for the New World on a ship named the *Mayflower.* The entire group of people who came on that ship came to be called Pilgrims, which means "religious wanderers."

The journey was very difficult. There were many storms, and the Pilgrims were very scared. They had to stay below deck. The rocking of the ship made many of them seasick. Finally, after two months at sea, they spotted land. The *Mayflower* was off the coast of Massachusetts.

This was not where the Pilgrims had planned to go, but they decided to make Massachusetts their new home. On December 11, 1620, they landed at Plymouth.

The winter in Plymouth was very hard. It was so cold that the men were not able to get the houses built. The Pilgrims had to stay on the ship. They were running out of the food that they had brought with them from England.

It was too late in the year to plant crops, and the Pilgrims didn't know how to hunt or fish. They grew weak from hunger and began to get sick. Many died. When spring arrived, only fifty-seven of the Pilgrims and only half of the crew of the *Mayflower* had survived.

Now that spring had come, the Pilgrims planted seeds. The crops that they had grown in England, however, did not grow well in the new land.

A Native American named Squanto saw this. He showed the Pilgrims how to plant corn, squash, beans, and pumpkins.

Squanto also showed the Pilgrims how to catch fish and the best places to catch them. He took the men hunting. He showed the children where to pick wild strawberries, cranberries, and gooseberries. Because of Squanto's help, that year's harvest produced more food than the Pilgrims thought possible.

In England, it was the custom to mark the end of the harvest with a big festival. The Pilgrims also wanted to give thanks to God for helping them survive the long journey from England and the hard winter. So they planned a big celebration with food and games for everyone. The Pilgrims invited their friend Squanto, who had done so much to help them have a good harvest. They asked him to bring some other Native Americans to the celebration.

Four married ladies, who were good cooks, were chosen to prepare the meal. The men set barrels in the middle of the only street in Plymouth. They set boards on the barrels and covered the boards with fine linen cloths. They also hunted the turkeys and ducks that the women cooked. Young women and children helped to do many things. They gathered berries, chopped vegetables, brought water, and gathered wood for fires to cook the food.

The meal probably included roasted deer meat; turkeys stuffed with nuts and dried fruits; boiled pumpkin (there was no flour or molasses to make pies); corn, which was made into a type of corn bread; cranberries, which were probably boiled to make a sauce;

and fish and seafood, such as eel and lobster.

Celebration day came and Squanto arrived, bringing ninety guests with him. The women were surprised; they had only prepared enough food for sixty people!

The Native Americans had brought deer and many turkeys to contribute to the feast.

The women cooked these and began cooking more food so that there would be enough for everyone.

They must have succeeded, because the celebration lasted for three days. Everyone ate, played games, sang, and danced.

People today do many of those same things when celebrating Thanksgiving. They get together with their families. They invite friends to celebrate with them. Usually there is a big meal with many of the same kinds of food the Pilgrims ate on the first Thanksgiving: turkey with stuffing, sweet potatoes, cranberries (made into sauce), and pumpkins (baked into pumpkin pies). Football is probably the most popular game for Thanksgiving today. People often gather to watch their favorite teams play. Some people like to play an informal game of touch football.

Because Thanksgiving is a time of sharing, it is often customary to share not just with friends and family, but with strangers who may be poor and hungry.

Volunteering to help at homeless shelters is a way many people spend Thanksgiving. For them, giving to others is a way to show thanks for all that they themselves have been given.

Every fall at Thanksgiving, people discover that there are almost as many ways to celebrate and show thanks as there are things to be thankful for. Just as the Pilgrims did, people take time to remember and give thanks for the blessings they have received.